CELEBRATING OUR HOLIDAYS

Celebrating DAY OF THE DEAD

By Elizabeth Morgan and Carol Gnojewski

Cavendish Square
New York

Published in 2023 by Cavendish Square Publishing, LLC
29 E. 21st Street New York, NY 10010

Website: cavendishsq.com

Library of Congress Cataloging-in-Publication Data

Names: Morgan, Elizabeth, author. | Gnojewski, Carol, author.
Title: Celebrating Day of the Dead / Elizabeth Morgan, Carol Gnojewski.
Description: New York : Cavendish Square Publishing, [2023] | Series:
Celebrating our holidays | Includes index.
Identifiers: LCCN 2021043577 | ISBN 9781502664938 (set) | ISBN
9781502664945 (library binding) | ISBN 9781502664921 (paperback) | ISBN
9781502664952 (ebook)
Subjects: LCSH: All Soul's Day–Juvenile literature. | Mexico–Social life
and customs–Juvenile literature.
Classification: LCC GT4995.A4 M67 2023 | DDC 394.266–dc23
LC record available at https://lccn.loc.gov/2021043577

Editor: Katie Kawa
Copyeditor: Jill Keppeler
Designer: Deanna Paternostro

The photographs in this book are used by permission and through the courtesy of: Cover, pp. 1, 23 AGCuesta/Shutterstock.com; back cover, pp. 3, 5, 7, 9, 12, 15, 17, 19, 22, 25, 27, 28, 29, 30, 31, 32 N.D.Vector/Shutterstock.com; pp. 4, 18, 21 Quetzalcoatl1/Shutterstock.com; p. 6 Kobby Dagan/Shutterstock.com; p. 7 Moab Republic/Shutterstock.com; p. 8 underworld/Shutterstock.com; p. 10 SL-Photography/Shutterstock.com; p. 11 Everett Collection/Shutterstock.com; p. 14 Cris_mh/Shutterstock.com; p. 16 Anton_Ivanov/Shutterstock.com; p. 17 Usa-Pyon/Shutterstock.com; p. 22 Victor Baril/Shutterstock.com; p. 24 Brandon Bourdages/Shutterstock.com; p. 26 Suriel Ramzal/Shutterstock.com; p. 28 TeaGraphicDesign/Shutterstock.com.

CPSIA compliance information: Batch #CSCSQ23: For further information contact Cavendish Square Publishing LLC, New York, New York, at 1-877-980-4450.

Printed in the United States of America

CONTENTS

Day of the Dead is celebrated on November 1 and 2 every year. In some places, celebrations begin on October 31, but midnight on November 1 is generally seen as the start of the holiday.

CHAPTER ONE

Día de los Muertos

People from different **cultures** often celebrate different holidays. Learning about those holidays can help us learn more about what's important to different groups of people. For example, people from Mexico and, to some extent, **Latin America** in general, celebrate a holiday called Día de los Muertos, or Day of the Dead. When people think of this holiday, they often think of **skulls**, flowers, and fancy altars. The meanings behind all these parts of the holiday show what's really important to the people who celebrate it—and that includes faith and family.

Cemetery Celebrations

Some people might think a **cemetery** is a creepy place to spend a holiday, but this location is at the center of Day of the Dead celebrations. This is because this holiday honors those who've died. It's believed that during this holiday, the souls of the dead can visit the world of the living again.

Day of the Dead isn't a sad or scary holiday. In fact, it's a time of happiness and peace. While people from some cultures, including many people from the United States, don't feel comfortable

Family members clean and decorate the graves of their loved ones for Day of the Dead. They then spend time celebrating in the cemetery with other families and friends.

talking about death or spending too much time in a cemetery, many Mexicans and others who celebrate Day of the Dead see death as part of the journey everyone must take, so it's not something to be afraid of. Instead, this holiday is celebrated with laughter and happy stories about family members who've died. This is a way of keeping their memory alive.

Growing in Popularity

Day of the Dead isn't a new holiday. Its roots reach far back into Mexican history. However, it's become more popular in the United States in recent years, especially as more **immigrants** from Mexico have come to the country. They've brought many **traditions** with them, including their Day of the Dead traditions.

Two Kinds of Traditions

Although Day of the Dead isn't the same thing as Halloween, some Halloween traditions have become part of Day of the Dead celebrations. For example, trick-or-treating has become a beloved part of Day of the Dead for some children. This is especially true for people who celebrate Day of the Dead in the United States, where Halloween is still the more popular holiday. Children go door to door asking for candy before the more traditional celebrations begin.

Even people who don't celebrate this holiday might recognize some of its traditions, including decorations and treats that look like skulls and skeletons (known as *calaveras* in Spanish) and skull masks (known as *calacas*) worn by some people. People often paint their faces to look like skulls for this holiday, and that tradition has become a common sight on the U.S. holiday of Halloween too.

Although Halloween, which is celebrated on October 31, may seem similar to Day of the Dead and is held around the same time, Day of the Dead isn't simply the Mexican Halloween. It's a special celebration with its own traditions, foods, meaning, and history.

Skulls are an important symbol, or sign, of Day of the Dead.

Both Mictlantecuhtli and Mictecacíhuatl have been shown in art as skeletons or as figures with a skull for a face. Shown here is a sculpture of Mictlantecuhtli.

Most souls, however, were sent to Mictlan. This was the Aztec underworld. The god of death, Mictlantecuhtli, was the ruler of Mictlan, along with his wife, Mictecacíhuatl. The journey a soul had to take through the underworld was long. There were nine parts to Mictlan, and a soul took four years to pass through them. Only in the last of the nine parts could they find rest.

This belief in the spirits of the dead and their journey through the afterlife is a big part of Day of the Dead. The Aztecs believed in burying the dead with objects that might help them on their journey through

Mictlan, which is similar to today's tradition of putting out food and other important items for the spirits on Day of the Dead.

The Spanish Take Over

The Aztec Empire ruled over what's now part of Mexico for many years—from the 1400s to the 1500s. By 1521, however, Spanish soldiers had

Shown here is an artist's idea of what it looked like when the Spanish, led by Hernán Cortés, encountered the Aztecs in Mexico.

arrived, overthrown the Aztec Empire, and taken over the Aztec cities. Mexico became a Spanish colony. Many Aztecs were enslaved. The Spanish wanted to get rid of the Aztec way of life. They brought in priests called missionaries. Missionaries taught the Aztecs about the Catholic religion, or belief system. Catholics believe in one god instead of many.

The Spanish wanted to replace the Aztecs' ancient beliefs with their religion. They tore down Aztec temples and built Catholic churches. They also wanted the Aztec people to celebrate Catholic holidays. Two such holidays were for honoring the dead.

Two Days of Celebrating

Day of the Dead actually lasts for two days—the same two days as All Saints' Day and All Souls' Day. In Mexico and other places where people celebrate Day of the Dead, November 1 is the day to remember children who've died. November 2 is the day to honor adults who've died. The **overlapping** of these special days shows the mixing of Catholic and indigenous, or native, beliefs, which was more common in Latin America than it was in the British North American colonies that became the United States.

Saints and Souls

Spanish Catholics celebrated two important days in November to honor those who had died. These days are still celebrated by Catholics today. November 1 is All Saints' Day. This is a day to celebrate and pray to all the saints—very holy people who've died. November 2 is

All Souls' Day. On this day, Catholics pray for the souls of all their loved ones who've died, especially those thought to be in a part of the afterlife known as purgatory. This is a place souls are believed to go before going to heaven.

Mexico became independent from Spain in 1821. For 300 years, many indigenous Mexican peoples had tried to keep their beliefs separate from those of the Spanish. However, over time, Spanish and indigenous traditions blended together. This can be seen in the celebration of Day of the Dead, which combines some Aztec beliefs and Spanish Catholic beliefs.

Today, each region, or part, of Mexico has different ways of celebrating Day of the Dead. One common practice is the making of an *ofrenda*, or altar. Ofrendas give families the chance to remember those who've died. They serve as a way to connect the living with the dead, which was important to both the Aztec people and the Spanish.

Ofrendas are seen throughout Mexico on November 1 and 2. They've also become more common in other countries too, especially the United States.

CHAPTER THREE

DAY OF THE DEAD TODAY

Day of the Dead is a holiday connected to ancient Aztec beliefs and Catholic traditions that are more than a thousand years old. However, it's still popular today—and it's popular in many places beyond the Mexican lands where it first began. People sometimes celebrate Day of the Dead in the United States. This holiday has grown in popularity as Mexican immigrants have traveled to new places and as books, movies, and other **media** have put Day of the Dead in the spotlight.

SPREADING THROUGHOUT MEXICO

Day of the Dead is celebrated throughout Mexico today, but that wasn't always the case. It started in the southern parts of the country, and it took a long time to catch on in the north. Even today, every Mexican city and rural community celebrates this holiday differently. Some cities hold parades, while celebrations in the countryside are sometimes smaller and quieter.

As the holiday grew throughout Mexico, it became one of the defining cultural events in the country. In fact, in 2008, it became part of UNESCO's Intangible Cultural Heritage list. This list includes kinds of storytelling, the skills and methods behind different arts and crafts, and holiday traditions. It's a way to show

UNESCO is a part of the United Nations (UN) that deals with global culture. It highlighted the importance of Day of the Dead for indigenous peoples when it added these celebrations to its Intangible Cultural Heritage list.

some of the most important cultural traditions from around the world, and Day of the Dead is now a part of that list.

Beyond Borders

In the 21st century, people celebrate Day of the Dead around the world. Mexican immigrants took this holiday with them to the places where they settled, and similar celebrations caught on in other parts of Latin America too.

Day of the Dead is now a popular holiday in many parts of the United States, especially parts with large Mexican communities. Cities

Keeping Culture Close

Day of the Dead traditions are an important way for Mexican Americans to keep their culture close in their new country. This is especially important because life isn't always easy for immigrants from Mexico and other Latin American countries. People are sometimes unkind to immigrants, and this can make immigrants feel unwelcome. It's good to help immigrants feel respected and accepted, and one of the best ways to do this is by respecting how they express their culture, including their holidays.

including Los Angeles, California, and Chicago, Illinois, have Day of the Dead celebrations. Museums, cultural centers, and even Walt Disney World in Florida have exhibits where people can learn more about this holiday.

Celebrating Day of the Dead is a way for people to feel united, even when they're far from home. For Mexican immigrants in the United States, it's a way to stay connected to their past even as they build a future in their new country. It's also a way to show their pride in their culture and to share that culture with their neighbors.

Many big cities across the United States have Day of the Dead celebrations.

Some people believe the spirits of their loved ones visit them during Day of the Dead. They decorate their ofrendas with things that will make the spirits happy when they visit.

CHAPTER FOUR

WHAT'S ON AN OFRENDA?

Day of the Dead traditions may not always look the same depending on where in the world they're happening. However, one important part of this holiday is shared by most people who celebrate it. That's the ofrenda. Families set up this special altar to honor their loved ones who've died, and they decorate it in ways that keep their memory alive.

A SPACE FOR THE DEAD

Every ofrenda tells a story about the person or people it honors. Things they liked or that belonged to them are placed on the altar. For example, if a dead relative loved to read, their favorite book might be added to the ofrenda. If families have pictures of their relatives who've died, these are also added to the ofrenda, along with candles and religious items such as statues.

The ofrenda creates a space for the dead in a family's daily life. Dead relatives seem closer when memories about them are shared. By making an ofrenda, families show how much their loved ones still mean to them. Children learn their family history this way.

People sometimes set up ofrendas outside the home too. Some are placed near graves or at the place where a person died. In central Mexico, some people build them on boats. They float them down the canals. Some large ofrendas are placed in town squares, churches, and government buildings. These ofrendas might be used to call attention to people who died because of crime, **poverty**, or unsafe working conditions. They can also honor those who might be forgotten, including **orphans** and those in prison.

The Meaning of the Marigolds

Most ofrendas—from the smallest household ones to ones placed in big buildings in important cities—are decorated with flowers. Mexican marigolds, or *cempasúchitl*, are known as the flower of the dead. During Day of the Dead celebrations, marigolds are placed in vases, planted near graves, and strung onto wreaths or arches. The arches are said to form a door for the dead to enter.

Flower petals also are scattered over graves, and some families make a path of petals from the cemetery to their home. They expect the spirits to follow this path. The scent of marigolds is said to be strong enough to be smelled from the afterlife, helping spirits to find their way back home for this holiday.

Food and Family

Food is an important part of many holidays, and Day of the Dead is no different. Food is present on most ofrendas. Families remember what their loved ones liked to eat, and they often make these dishes to please the spirits they believe will visit during this holiday. Some kind of drink is left on the ofrenda, too, in case the spirits are thirsty when they arrive.

No offering to the spirits is complete without *pan de muerto*, or bread of the dead. This sweet egg bread is flavored with cinnamon, orange, or anise, which tastes like black licorice. The bread is then

Marigolds are brightly colored—often a kind of orange-yellow. Some people believe this helps them to be seen by the spirits from the afterlife.

glazed with honey or sprinkled with sugar. Sometimes the loaves are shaped like people or animals. A popular pan de muerto shape is that of a skull.

Offerings of food are said to make spirits feel welcome in the homes of the living. The dead can't really eat the food, but they're thought to take in its wonderful smell. When the spirits leave, families make a meal of what's left on the altar.

Pretty Paper

One of the most colorful parts of Day of the Dead is the use of *papel picado* to decorate ofrendas and other areas of cities and towns for this special day. Papel picado is a special kind of paper craft in which beautiful **designs** are cut into tissue paper of many different colors. It's a Mexican art form that's used for many different holidays and celebrations, including Day of the Dead.

Papel picado is a popular kind of decoration for Day of the Dead.

Shown here is part of an ofrenda featuring pan de muerto. This sweet treat is a popular Day of the Dead food.

Families often share food with each other during this holiday. This is especially true when they gather at the cemetery. They share meals, stories, and music as they celebrate this special pair of days.

Day of the Dead skulls are often colorful and pretty—not scary or spooky!

CHAPTER FIVE

SKULLS, SKELETONS, AND SONGS

Skulls and skeletons are common sights during Day of the Dead. They represent, or stand for, the dead who are honored during this holiday, and they are also connected to the Aztecs and their beliefs. Skulls and skeletons show up in many creative places during this holiday. They can be toys, artwork, and even candies!

CELEBRATING WITH CALAVERAS

Some of the skeletons and skulls seen across Mexico on this holiday are based on the work of an artist named José Guadalupe Posada. Posada lived and worked in Mexico during the late 1800s. His art was sometimes printed in newspapers. Posada drew many different kinds of calaveras. He often used these calaveras to make a point about Mexican government and culture.

Today, images of skulls and skeletons are fun parts of Day of the Dead celebrations. They're sometimes shown doing activities that people who've died might have done when they were alive, such as riding a horse or playing a guitar. These skeletons are popular toys for the holiday, and skulls are popular decorations around Mexican homes at this time of year.

Sugar Skulls

Skulls made out of sugar are also important parts of Day of the Dead celebrations. Sugar skulls are often given as gifts. Families also place them on the graves of young children or ofrendas after a child has died.

Sugar skulls are another way to connect Day of the Dead to Mexico's Aztec past. Stacked on candy-store shelves, rows of sugar skulls look something like *tzompantli*. These were racks that Aztecs used to dry out human skulls. Holes were drilled through the skulls so that they could be strung side by side on wooden rods like beads. Although sugar skulls might look like real skulls, they're just tasty treats and nothing to be afraid of.

Sugar skulls can be painted in bright colors and decorated in very fancy ways.

An Animated Adventure

Many kids today know about Day of the Dead because of *Coco*—a Disney movie created by Pixar Animation Studios. It came out in 2017 and tells the story of Miguel, a boy who travels to the Land of the Dead and must find his way home before the Day of the Dead celebrations are done. Many important parts of this holiday are in the film, including ofrendas, skulls and skeletons, and music. It also shows the importance of family and how this holiday keeps the memories of deceased, or dead, loved ones alive.

Celebrating with Your Senses

Songs and poems play a big part in Day of the Dead celebrations for many Mexicans and others who celebrate this holiday. A fun part of Day of the Dead is the writing and reading of funny poems called *calaveras literarias*. These poems often poke fun at government leaders and other famous people.

In addition to poems, music is a popular part of Day of the Dead. It can be heard coming from homes, town squares, and cemeteries throughout this holiday. With music in the air, special foods on the stove, the scent of marigolds leading the way for the spirits, and the sight of beautiful ofrendas paying tribute to those who've died, Day of the Dead is a true feast for the senses. It's a time to remember the dead—not with sadness but with joy, laughter, and love.

HOLIDAY HOW-TO

Make Sugar Skulls Out of Stone

You Will Need:

clean stones, each in the general shape of a skull (ovals or circles can work well)

acrylic paint in black, white, and a number of other colors

paintbrushes

old newspaper

covering for clothes

This is one kind of sugar skull design you can use, but you can paint your stones any way you want!

Directions:

1. Cover your workspace in old newspaper and your clothes in something that can get dirty, such as overalls or an old shirt, so the paint won't stain anything.
2. Paint a white skull shape on your first stone, and let it dry.
3. Add features to your skull, such as an upside-down heart for a nose, a big mouth, and a crown of marigolds. You can choose how you want your skull to look!
4. Repeat steps 2 and 3 with other stones if you want to make more skulls.
5. Decorate your garden, porch, or any other area of your home with your stones around November 1 and 2.

GLOSSARY

acrylic: Relating to a kind of paint used by artists and made from a certain chemical process.

cemetery: A place where dead people are buried.

culture: The beliefs and ways of life of a certain group of people.

design: A decorative pattern. Also, a drawing of something that is being planned or created.

immigrant: A person who comes to a country to live there.

Latin America: All the Americas south of the United States.

media: The systems and ways of communication that are used to inform a large number of people.

orphan: A child whose parents are dead.

overlap: To happen at the same time as something else.

poverty: The state of being poor.

skull: The bones that form the head and face of a person or animal.

tradition: A way of thinking, behaving, or doing something that's been used by people in a particular society for a long time.

United Nations: An organization formed in 1945 to promote international cooperation.

FIND OUT MORE

Books

Hutchinson, Patricia. *Day of the Dead*. Minneapolis, MN: ABDO Publishing, 2021.

Shofner, Melissa Raé. *The Story Behind Day of the Dead*. New York, NY: PowerKids Press, 2020.

Vallepur, Shalini. *Day of the Dead*. King's Lynn, UK: BookLife Publishing, 2021.

Websites

Day of the Dead and the Sugar Skull
www.cbc.ca/kidscbc2/the-feed/day-of-the-dead-and-the-sugar-skull
Visitors to this website will find answers to important questions about Day of the Dead, as well as a link to make their own skull mask.

***National Geographic Kids*: Day of the Dead**
kids.nationalgeographic.com/celebrations/article/day-of-the-dead
This website introduces kids to basic facts about Day of the Dead and features colorful pictures of celebrations.

INDEX